Impressum
Verlag: BABADADA GmbH, Nedderfeld 112 , 22529 Hamburg
Geschäftsführer / Verlagsleitung: Harald Hof
Druck: Books on Demand GmbH, In de Tarpen 42, 22848 Norderstedt

Imprint
Publisher: BABADADA GmbH, Nedderfeld 112 , 22529 Hamburg, Germany
Managing Director / Publishing direction: Harald Hof
Print: Books on Demand GmbH, In de Tarpen 42, 22848 Norderstedt

school

学校

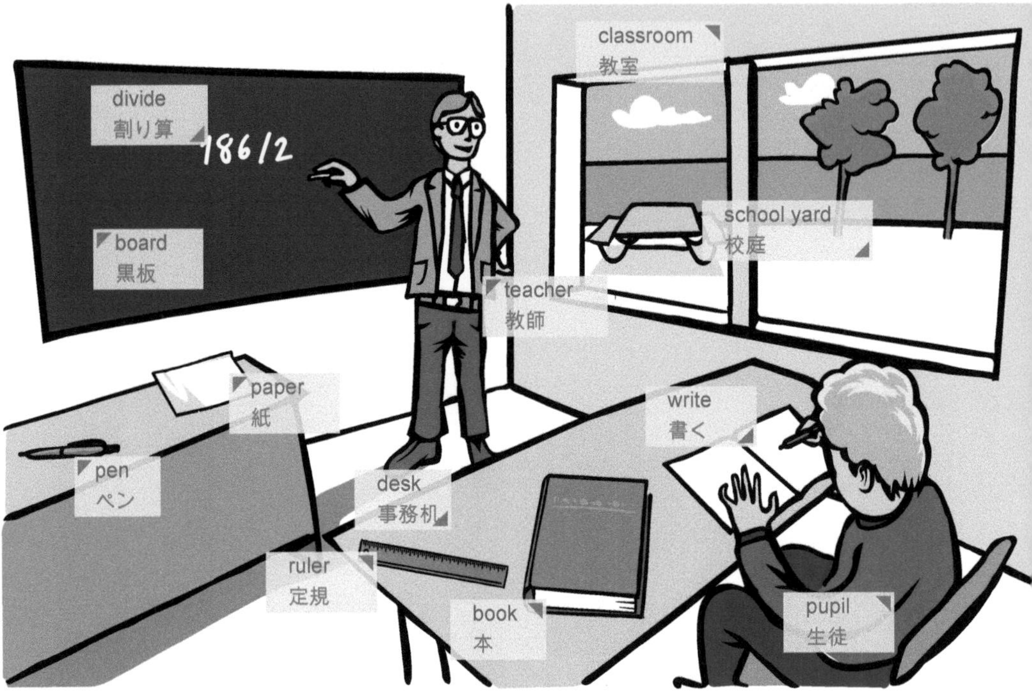

classroom
教室
divide
割り算
186/2
board
黒板
school yard
校庭
teacher
教師
paper
紙
write
書く
pen
ペン
desk
事務机
ruler
定規
book
本
pupil
生徒

satchel
ランドセル

pencil case
筆入れ

pencil
鉛筆

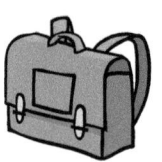

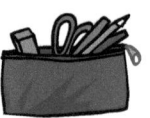

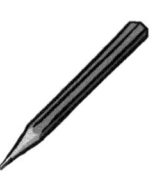

pencil sharpener
鉛筆削り

rubber
消しゴム

drawing pad
スケッチブック

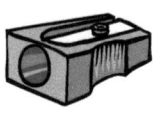

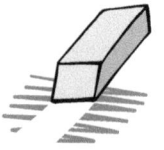

drawing
スケッチ

paintbrush
絵筆

paint box
絵の具箱

scissors
はさみ

glue
接着剤

exercise book
練習帳

homework
宿題

number
数

add
足し算

subtract
引き算

multiply
かけ算

calculate
計算する

letter
文字

alphabet
アルファベット

word
単語

text

テキスト

read

読む

chalk

チョーク

lesson

授業

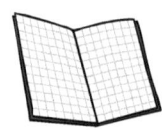

register

学級日誌

exam

試験

certificate

通知表

school uniform

制服

education

教育

encyclopedia

百科事典

university

大学

microscope

顕微鏡

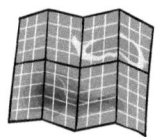

map

地図

waste-paper basket

ごみ箱

travel
旅行

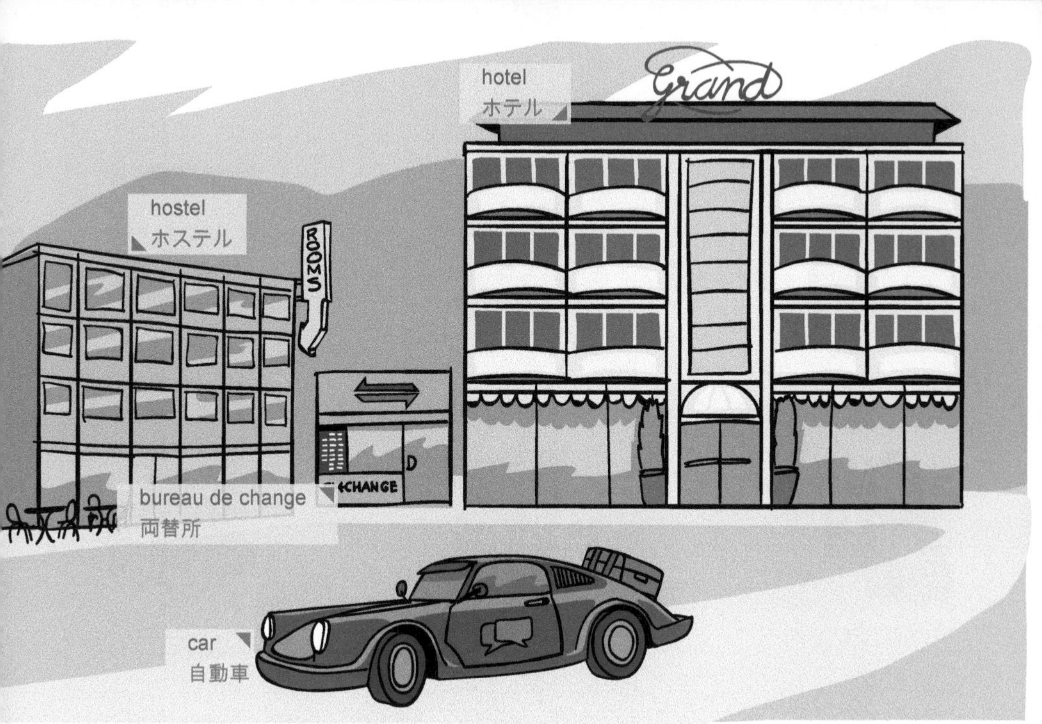

hotel
ホテル
Grand
hostel
ホステル
ROOMS
CHANGE
bureau de change
両替所
car
自動車

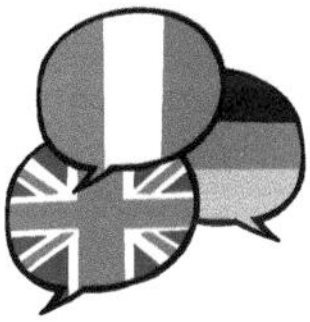

language

言語

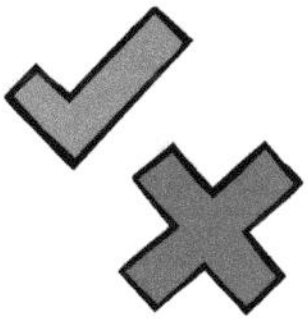

yes / no

はい / いいえ

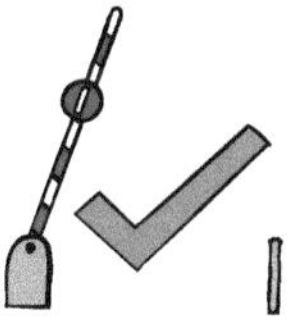

Okay

問題ない

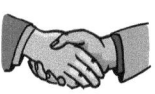

hello

ハロー

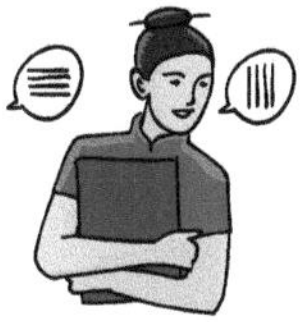

translator

翻訳者

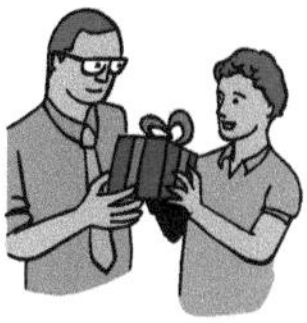

Thank you

ありがとう

how much is...?

...はいくらですか？

I do not understand

わかりません

problem

問題

Good evening!

こんばんは！

Good morning!

おはようございます！

Good night!

おやすみなさい！

bye bye

さようなら

direction

方向

luggage

手荷物

bag

バッグ

backpack

リュックサック

guest

お客様

room

部屋

sleeping bag

寝袋

tent

テント

tourist information
旅行者情報

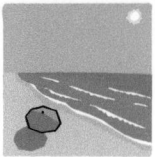

beach
ビーチ

credit card
クレジットカード

breakfast
朝食

lunch
昼食

dinner
夕食

ticket
チケット

lift
エレベーター

stamp
スタンプ

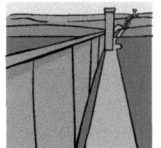

border
境界

customs
税関

embassy
大使館

visa
ビザ

passport
パスポート

travel - 旅行

transport
輸送

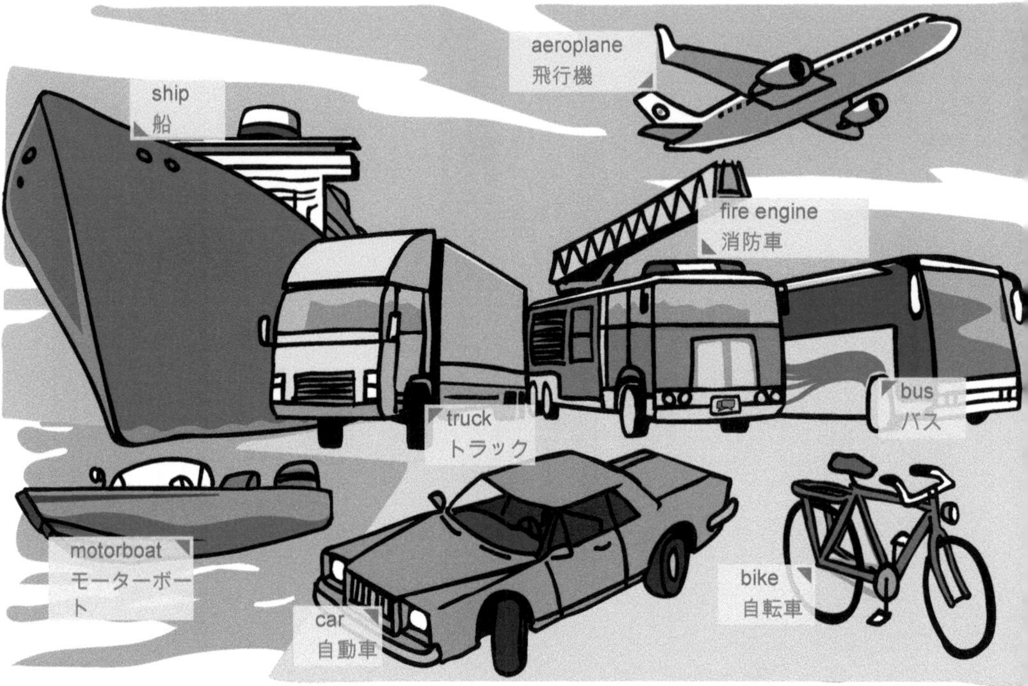

aeroplane
飛行機
ship
船
fire engine
消防車
truck
トラック
bus
バス
motorboat
モーターボー
ト
bike
自転車
car
自動車

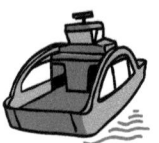

ferry
フェリー

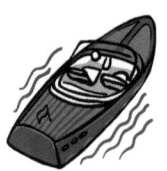

boat
ボート

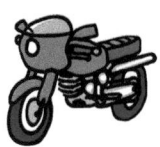

motorbike
バイク

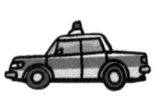

police car
パトカー

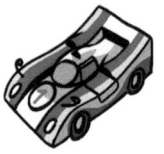

racing car
レーシングカー

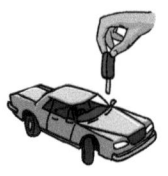

rental car
レンタカー

car sharing

カーシェアリング

breakdown truck

レッカー車

refuse truck

ごみ収集車

motor

モーター

fuel

燃料

petrol station

ガソリンスタンド

traffic sign

交通標識

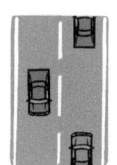

traffic

交通

traffic jam

渋滞

car park

駐車場

train station

駅

tracks

道

train

列車

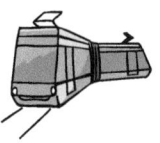

tram

路面電車

carriage

車両

helicopter

ヘリコプター

airport

空港

tower

タワー

passenger

乗客

container

コンテナ

carton

段ボール箱

cart

カート

basket

カゴ

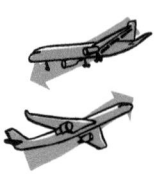

take off / land

離陸 / 着陸

city

都市

village

村

city centre

都心

house

家

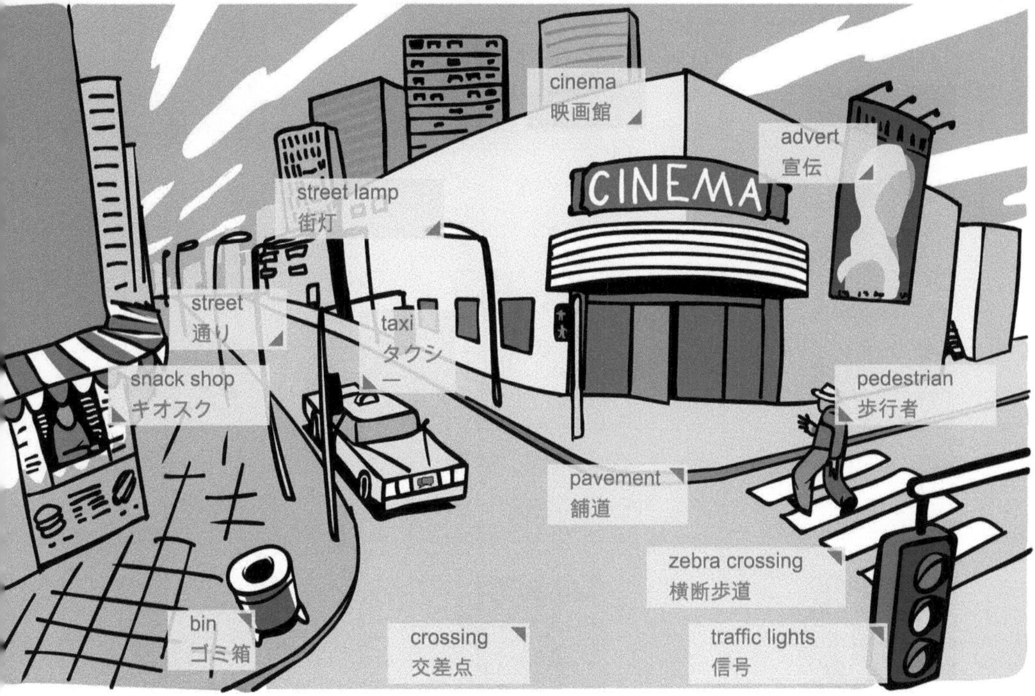
cinema
映画館
advert
宣伝
street lamp
街灯
street
通り
taxi
タクシー
snack shop
キオスク
pedestrian
歩行者
pavement
舗道
zebra crossing
横断歩道
bin
ゴミ箱
crossing
交差点
traffic lights
信号

hut
小屋

flat
アパート

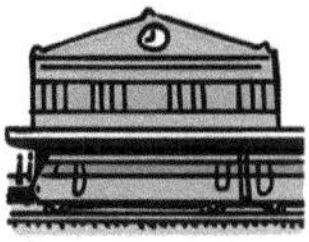
train station
駅

town hall
市役所

museum
美術館

school
学校

university

大学

bank

銀行

hospital

病院

hotel

ホテル

pharmacy

薬局

office

オフィス

book shop

書店

shop

ショップ

florist's

花屋

supermarket

スーパーマーケット

market

市場

department store

デパート

fishmonger's

魚屋

shopping centre

ショッピングセンター

harbour

港

park
公園

bench
ベンチ

bridge
橋

stairs
階段

underground
地下鉄

tunnel
トンネル

bus stop
バス停

bar
バー

restaurant
レストラン

postbox
ポスト

street sign
道路標識

parking meter
パーキングメーター

zoo
動物園

swimming pool
スイミングプール

mosque
モスク

farm
....
農場

pollution
....
汚染

graveyard
....
墓地

church
....
教会

playground
....
遊び場

temple
....
寺

landscape
風景

signpost
道標

way
道

meadow
草地

stone
石

tree
木

hiker
ハイカー

river
川

grass
草

flower
花

valley

谷

hill

山

lake

湖

forest

森

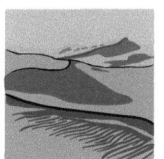

desert

砂漠

volcano

火山

castle

城

rainbow

虹

mushroom

キノコ

palm tree

ヤシの木

mosquito

蚊

fly

ハエ

ant

蟻

bee

ミツバチ

spider

クモ

landscape - 風景

beetle

カブトムシ

frog

蛙

squirrel

リス

hedgehog

ハリネズミ

hare

ウサギ

owl

フクロウ

bird

鳥

swan

白鳥

boar

雄豚

deer

鹿

moose

ヘラジカ

dam

ダム

wind turbine

風力タービン

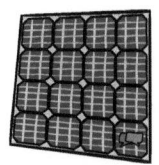

solar panel

ソーラーパネル

climate

気候

restaurant
レストラン

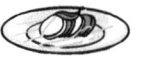

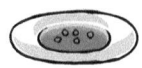

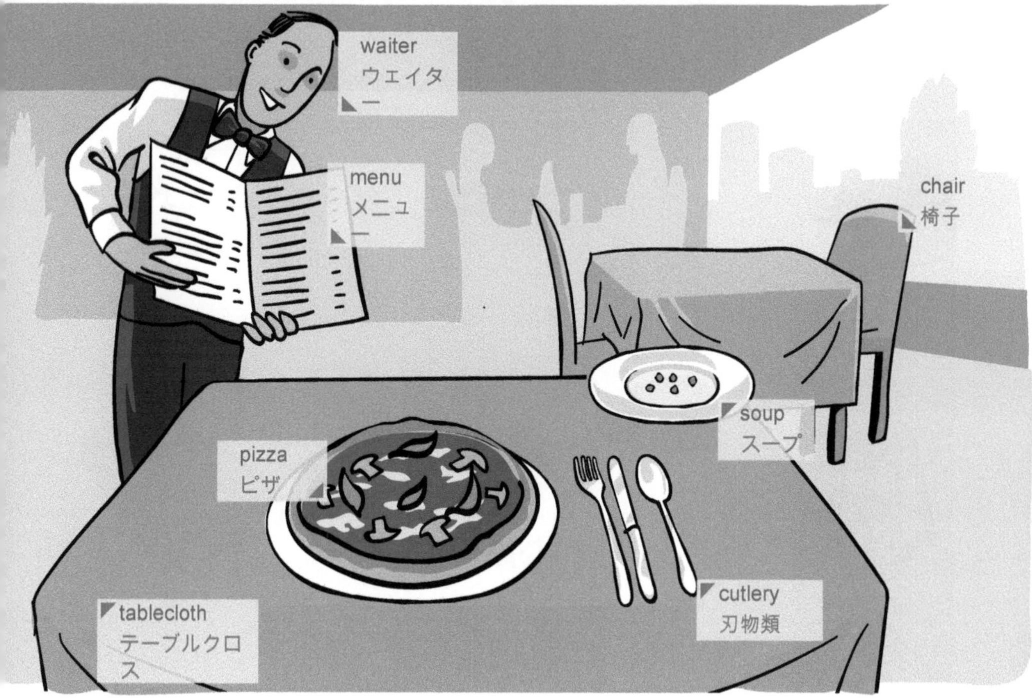
waiter
ウェイター
menu
メニュー
chair
椅子
soup
スープ
pizza
ピザ
cutlery
刃物類
tablecloth
テーブルクロス

starter

前菜

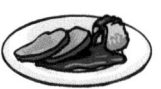

main course

メインコース

dessert

デザート

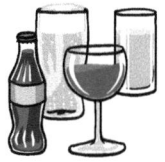

drinks

飲み物

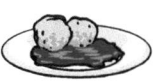

food

食べ物

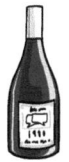

bottle

ボトル

fast food

ファストフード

street food

屋台の食べ物

teapot

ティーポット

sugar bowl

砂糖入れ

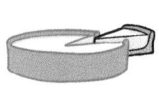

portion

一人前

espresso machine

エスプレッソマシン

high chair

幼児用食事椅子

bill

請求書

tray

トレー

knife

ナイフ

fork

フォーク

spoon

スプーン

teaspoon

ティースプーン

serviette

ナプキン

glass

グラス

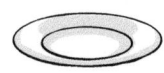

plate

皿

soup plate

スープ皿

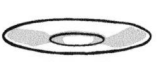

saucer

受け皿

sauce

ソース

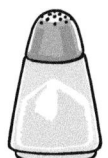

salt pot

塩入れ

pepper mill

ペッパーミル

vinegar

酢

oil

油

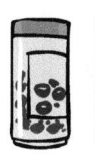

spices

スパイス

ketchup

ケチャップ

mustard

マスタード

mayonnaise

マヨネーズ

supermarket

スーパーマーケット

special offer
特価品
customer
顧客
dairy
乳製品
FOR
fruit
果物
trolley
ショッピング
・カート

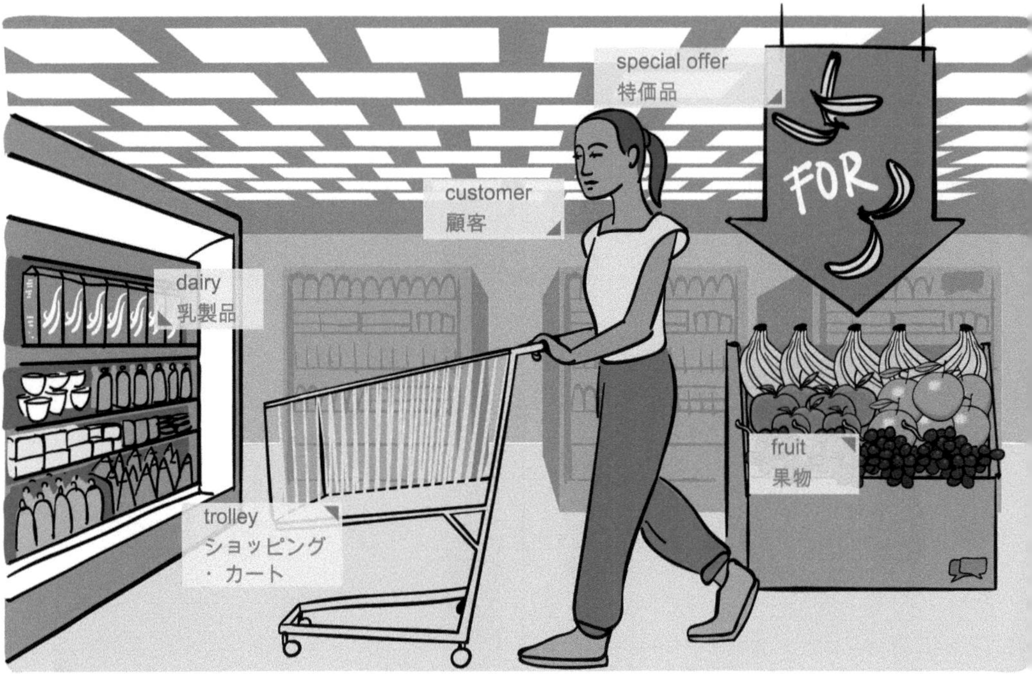

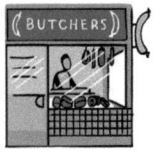

BUTCHERS

butcher´s

肉屋

BAKERY

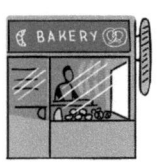

baker´s

パン屋

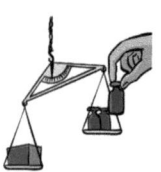

weigh

重さをはかる

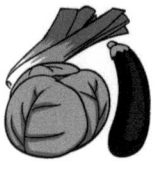

vegetables

野菜

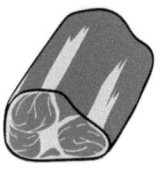

meat

肉

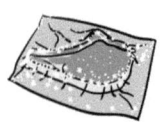

frozen food

冷凍食品

cold meat

冷肉の薄切り

tinned food

缶詰食品

washing powder

洗剤

sweets

菓子

household products

家庭用品

cleaning products

清掃用品

salesperson

販売員

till

現金箱

cashier

レジ係

shopping list

買い物リスト

opening hours

開館時刻

wallet

財布

credit card

クレジットカード

bag

バッグ

plastic bag

ポリ袋

water

水

juice

ジュース

milk

牛乳

coke

コーラ

wine

ワイン

beer

ビール

alcohol

アルコール

cocoa

ココア

tea

紅茶

coffee

コーヒー

espresso

エスプレッソ

cappuccino

カプチーノ

banana

バナナ

apple

リンゴ

orange

オレンジ

melon

メロン

lemon

レモン

carrot

ニンジン

garlic

ニンニク

bamboo

竹

onion

玉ねぎ

mushroom

キノコ

nuts

ナッツ

noodles

ヌードル

spaghetti

スパゲッティ

rice

米

salad

サラダ

chips

フライドポテト

fried potatoes

フライドポテト

pizza

ピザ

hamburger

ハンバーガー

sandwich

サンドウィッチ

cutlet

カツレツ

ham

ハム

salami

サラミ

sausage

ソーセージ

chicken

鶏肉

roast

焼き

fish

魚

food - 食べ物

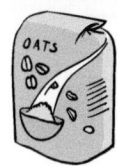

porridge oats

麦のお粥

muesli

ムーズリ

cornflakes

コーンフレーク

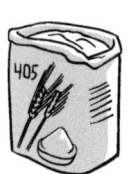

flour

小麦粉

croissant

クロワッサン

bread roll

ロールパン

bread

パン

toast

トースト

biscuits

ビスケット

butter

バター

curd

カッテージチーズ

cake

ケーキ

egg

卵

fried egg

目玉焼き

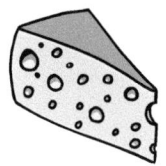

cheese

チーズ

ice cream

アイスクリーム

sugar

砂糖

honey

はちみつ

jam

ジャム

chocolate spread

ヌガークリーム

curry

カレー

farm
農場

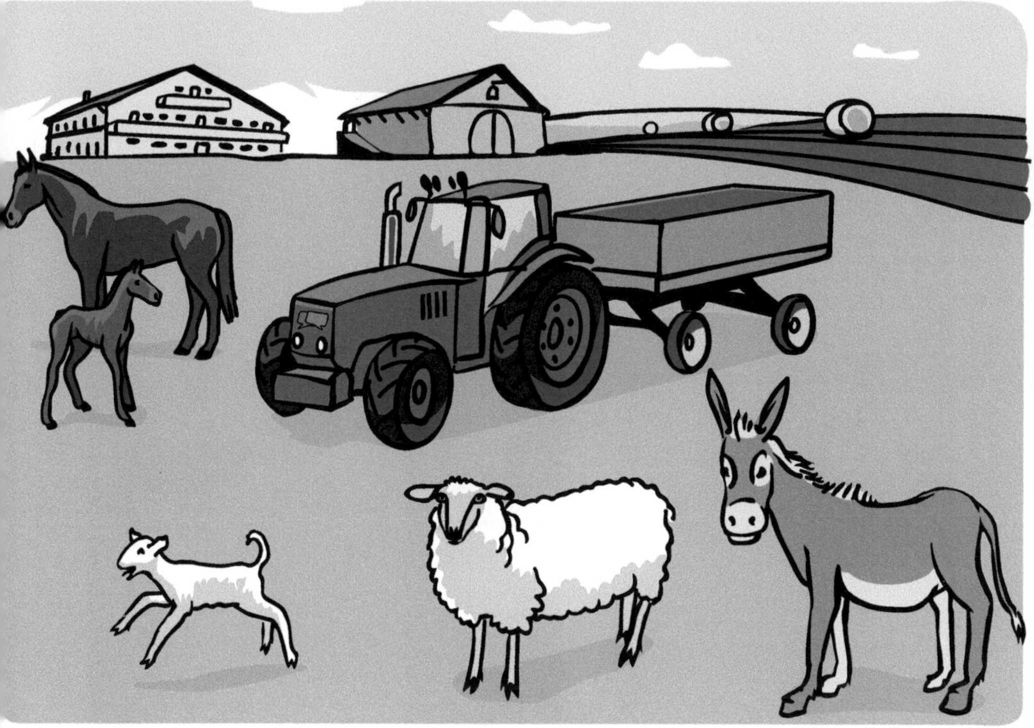

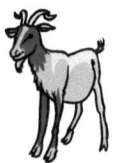

goat

ヤギ

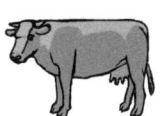

cow

雌牛

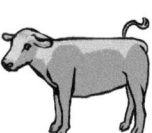

calf

子牛

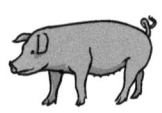

pig

豚

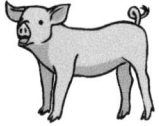

piglet

子豚

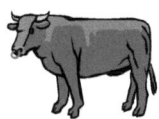

bull

雄牛

goose
ガチョウ

duck
アヒル

chick
ひよこ

hen
にわとり

cock
おんどり

rat
ネズミ

cat
猫

mouse
ねずみ

ox
雄牛

dog
犬

doghouse
犬小屋

garden hose
散水ホース

watering can
じょうろ

scythe
大鎌

plough
すき

sickle
草刈り鎌

hoe
くわ

pitchfork
堆肥用フォーク

axe
斧

wheelbarrow
手押し車

trough
かいばおけ

milk can
牛乳缶

sack
袋

fence
フェンス

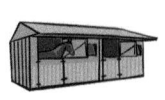
stable
畜舎

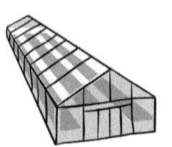
greenhouse
温室

soil
土壌

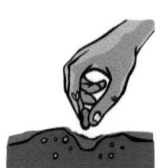
seed
種

fertilizer
肥料

combine harvester
コンバイン

harvest

収穫する

harvest

収穫

yams

ヤマイモ

wheat

小麦

soy

大豆

potato

じゃがいも

corn

トウモロコシ

rapeseed

菜種

fruit tree

果樹

cassava

キャッサバ

cereals

穀物

house

家

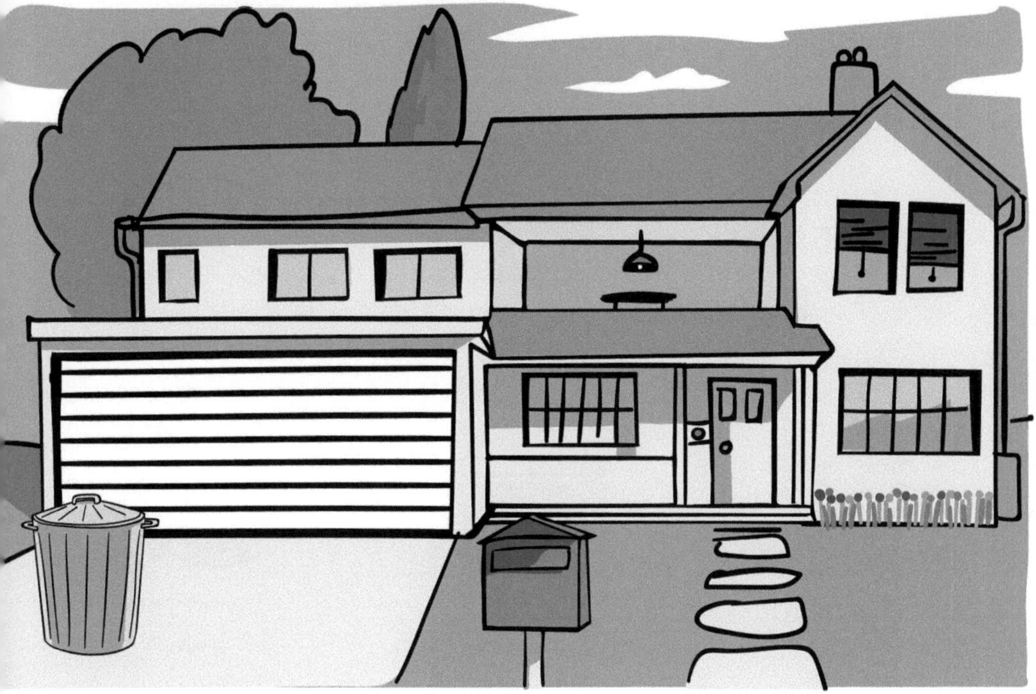

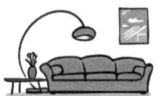

living room

リビングルーム

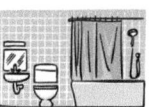

bathroom

浴室

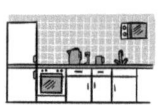

kitchen

台所

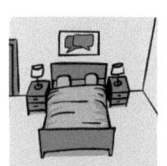

bedroom

寝室

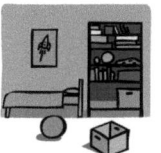

child's room

子供部屋

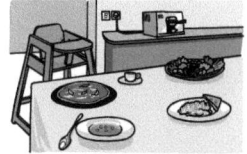

dining room

ダイニング・ルーム

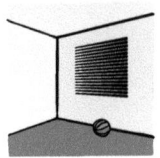

floor

床

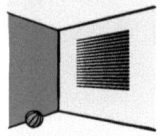

wall

壁

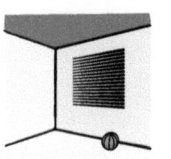

ceiling

天井

cellar

地下貯蔵庫

sauna

サウナ

balcony

バルコニー

terrace

テラス

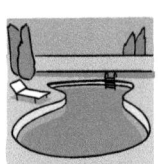

pool

プール

lawn mower

芝刈り機

sheet

シーツ

bedspread

ベッドカバー

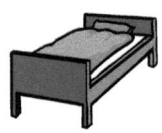

bed

ベッド

broom

ほうき

bucket

バケツ

switch

スイッチ

living room
リビングルーム

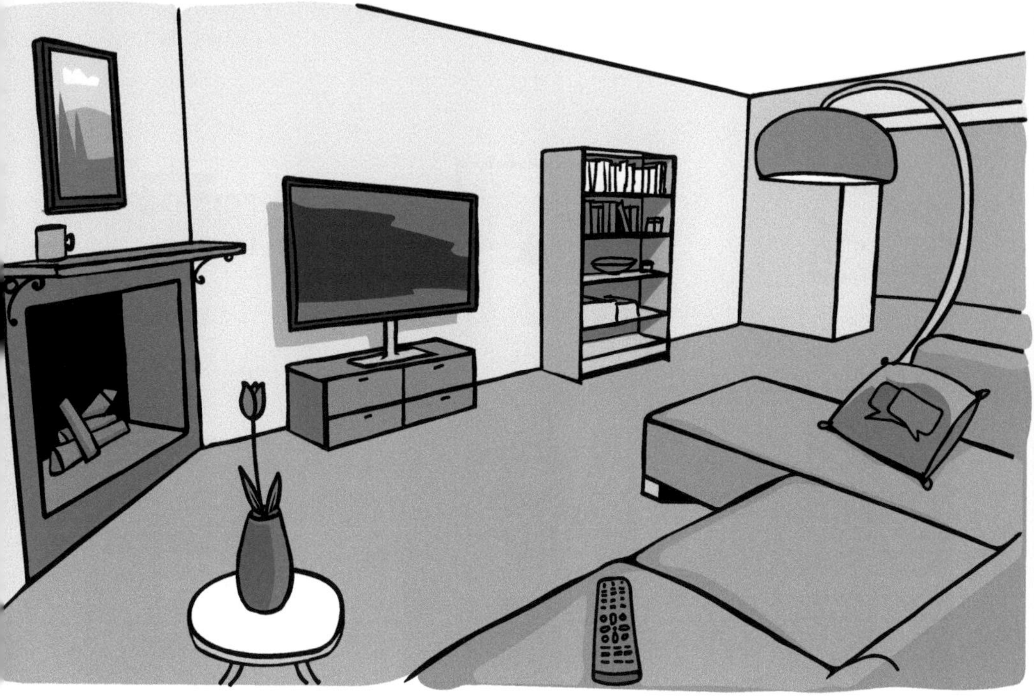

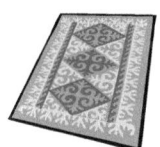

carpet

カーペット

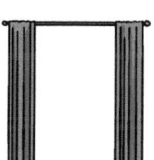

curtain

カーテン

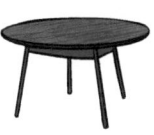

table

テーブル

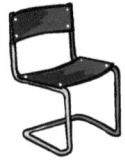

chair

椅子

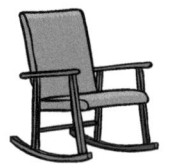

rocking chair

ロッキングチェア

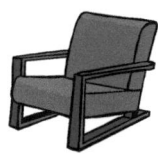

armchair

ひじ掛け椅子

book

本

blanket

毛布

decoration

飾り

firewood

たきぎ

film

映画

hi-fi equipment

ステレオ

key

鍵

newspaper

新聞

painting

絵画

poster

ポスター

radio

ラジオ

notepad

メモ帳

hoover

掃除機

cactus

サボテン

candle

ろうそく

kitchen
台所

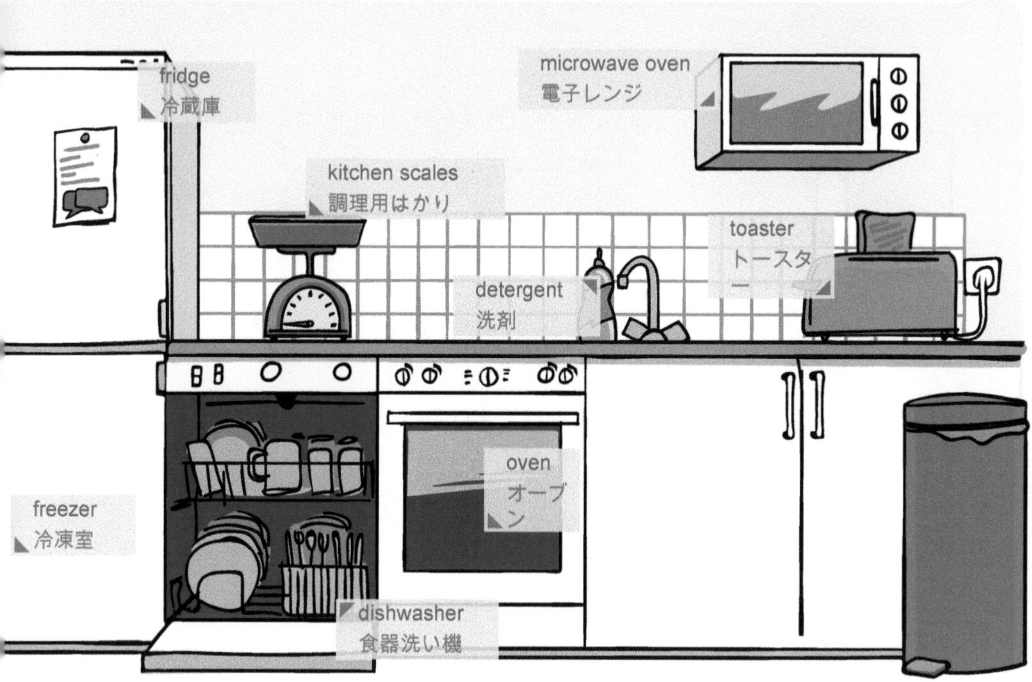
fridge
冷蔵庫
microwave oven
電子レンジ
kitchen scales
調理用はかり
toaster
トースター
detergent
洗剤
oven
オーブン
freezer
冷凍室
dishwasher
食器洗い機

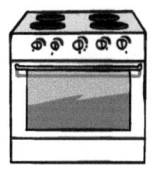

cooker
こんろ

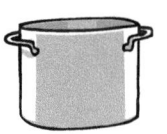

pot
鍋

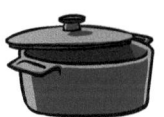

cast-iron pot
鉄鍋

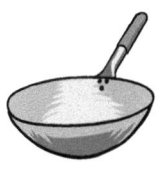

wok / kadai
中華鍋/ カダイ鍋

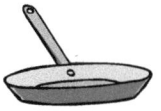

pan
フライパン

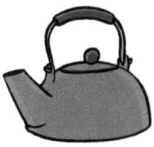

kettle
やかん

steamer

蒸し器

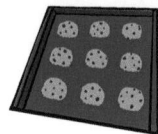

baking tray

天板

crockery

食器

mug

マグカップ

bowl

ボウル

chopsticks

箸

ladle

おたま

spatula

へら

whisk

泡立て器

strainer

こし器

sieve

ふるい

grater

すりおろし器

mortar

すり鉢

barbecue

バーベキュー

open fire

かまど

chopping board

まな板

rolling pin

麺棒

corkscrew

栓抜き

can

缶

can opener

缶切り

pot holder

鍋つかみ

sink

流し

brush

ブラシ

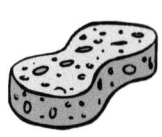

sponge

スポンジ

blender

ミキサー

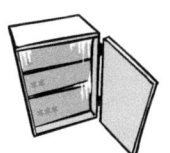

deep freezer

冷凍庫

baby bottle

哺乳瓶

tap

蛇口

bathroom

浴室

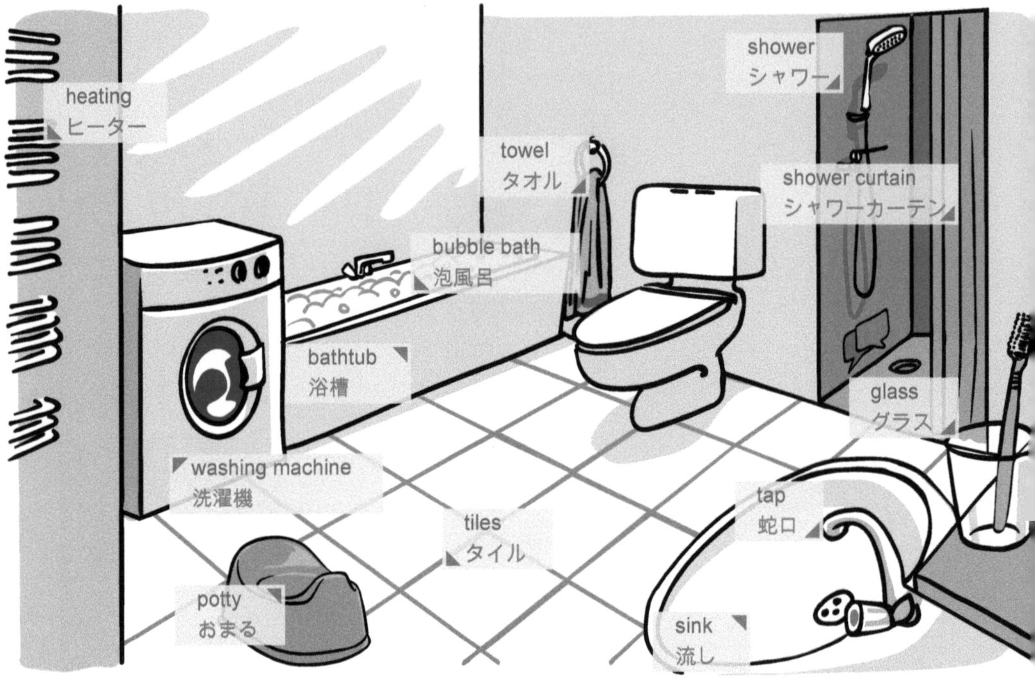

heating
ヒーター
shower
シャワー
towel
タオル
shower curtain
シャワーカーテン
bubble bath
泡風呂
bathtub
浴槽
glass
グラス
washing machine
洗濯機
tap
蛇口
tiles
タイル
potty
おまる
sink
流し

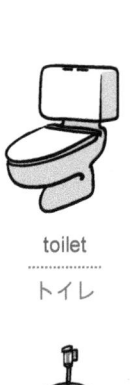

toilet

トイレ

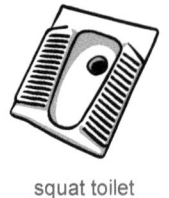

squat toilet

和式トイレ

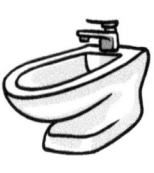

bidet

ビデ

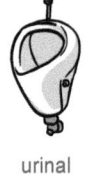

urinal

小便器

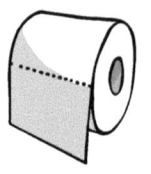

toilet paper

トイレットペーパー

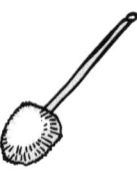

toilet brush

トイレブラシ

toothbrush

歯ブラシ

toothpaste

歯みがき

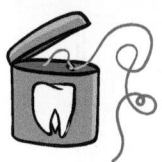

dental floss

デンタルフロス

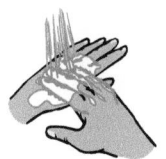

wash

洗う

handheld shower

シャワーヘッド

douche

ハンドビデ

basin

洗面台

back brush

ボディブラシ

soap

石鹸

shower gel

シャワー用ジェル

shampoo

シャンプー

flannel

浴用タオル

drain

排水口

cream

クリーム

deodorant

消臭

mirror

鏡

hand mirror

手鏡

razor

かみそり

shaving foam

シェービング・フォーム

aftershave

アフターシェーブローショ
ン

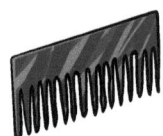

comb

櫛

brush

ブラシ

hair dryer

ドライヤー

hairspray

ヘアスプレー

makeup

化粧

lipstick

口紅

nail varnish

マニキュア

cotton wool

脱脂綿

nail scissors

爪切り

perfume

香水

washbag

洗面用具入れ

stool

スツール

weighing scale

体重計

bathrobe

バスローブ

rubber gloves

ゴム手袋

tampon

タンポン

sanitary towel

生理用ナプキン

chemical toilet

ケミカルトイレ

child's room
子供部屋

alarm clock
目覚まし時計
cuddly toy
ぬいぐるみ
toy car
おもちゃの
自動車
rattle
がらがら
doll's house
ドール・ハウス
present
プレゼン
ト

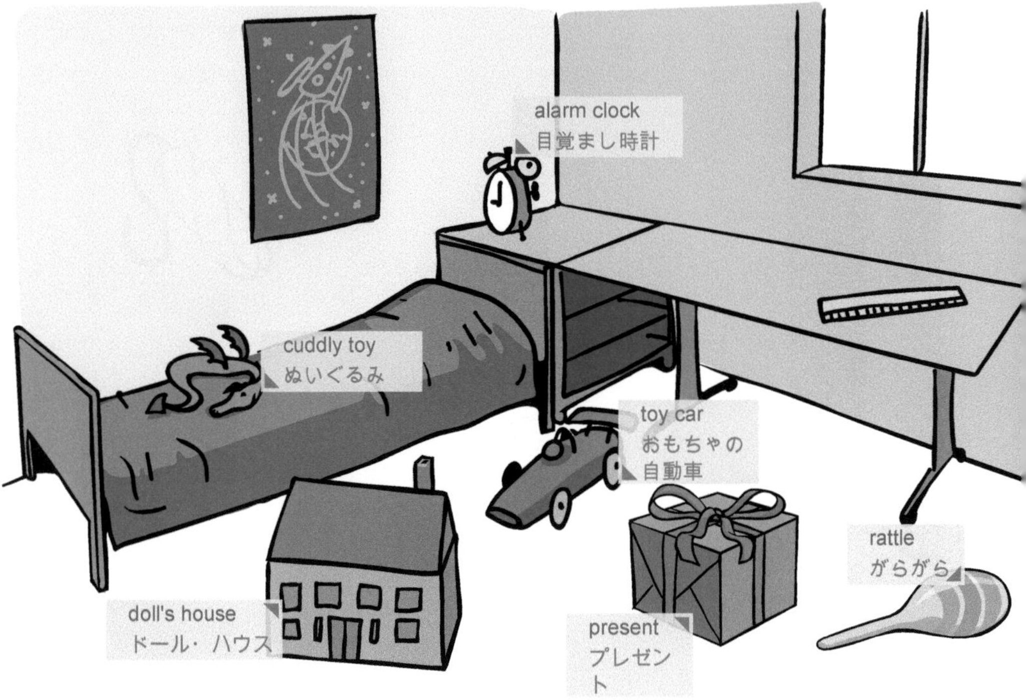

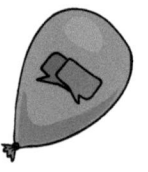

balloon
風船

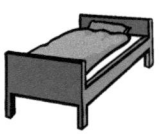

bed
ベッド

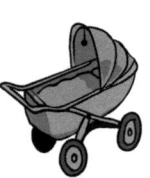

pram
ベビーカー

deck of cards
カードゲーム

jigsaw
ジグソーパズル

SUPER
MEGA

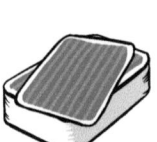

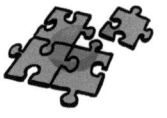

comic
漫画

lego bricks
レゴ

building blocks
玩具ブロック

action figure
アクションフィギュア

babygrow
ロンパース

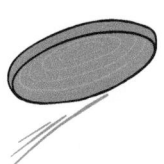

frisbee
フリスビー

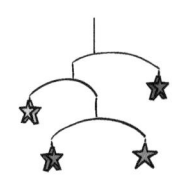

mobile
モバイル

board game
ボードゲーム

dice
さいころ

model train set
鉄道模型

dummy
おしゃぶり

party
パーティー

picture book
絵本

ball
ボール

doll
人形

play
遊ぶ

sandpit

砂場

swing

ブランコ

toys

おもちゃ

video game console

ゲーム機

tricycle

三輪車

teddy bear

テディベア

wardrobe

衣装ダンス

clothing

衣服

socks

靴下

stockings

ストッキング

tights

タイツ

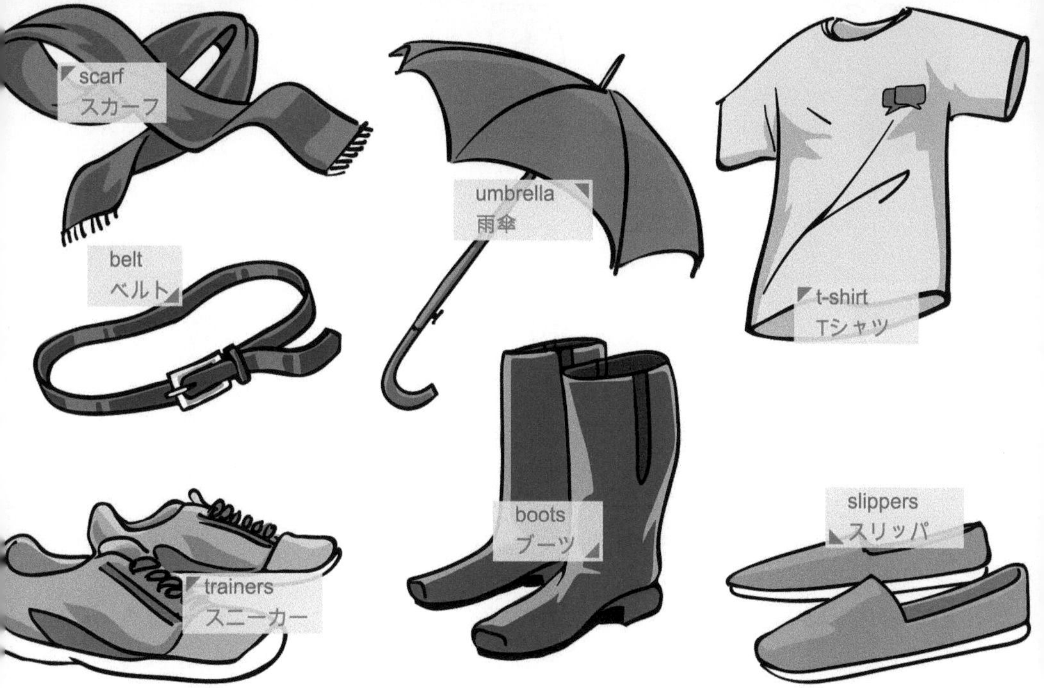

scarf
スカーフ

umbrella
雨傘

t-shirt
Tシャツ

belt
ベルト

boots
ブーツ

slippers
スリッパ

trainers
スニーカー

sandals

靴

sandals
サンダル

shoes
靴

rubber boots
ゴム長靴

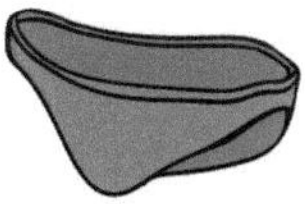

underpants
パンツ

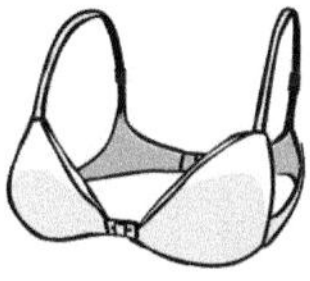

bra
ブラ

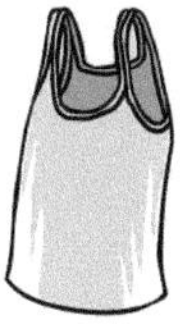

vest
ベスト

body

ボディースーツ

trousers

ズボン

jeans

ジーンズ

skirt

スカート

blouse

ブラウス

shirt

シャツ

pullover

セーター

hoodie

パーカー

blazer

ブレザー

jacket

ジャケット

coat

コート

raincoat

レインコート

costume

服装

dress

ドレス

wedding dress

ウェディングドレス

suit
スーツ

nightgown
ナイトガウン

pyjamas
パジャマ

sari
サリー

headscarf
ヘッドスカーフ

turban
ターバン

burqa
ブルカ

kaftan
カフタン

abaya
アバヤ

swimsuit
水着

trunks
トランクス

shorts
半ズボン

tracksuit
スウェットスーツ

apron
エプロン

gloves
手袋

button

ボタン

glasses

メガネ

bracelet

ブレスレット

necklace

ネックレス

ring

指輪

earring

イヤリング

cap

帽子

coat hanger

ハンガー

hat

帽子

tie

ネクタイ

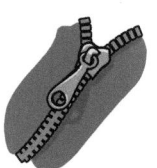

zip

ファスナー

helmet

ヘルメット

braces

サスペンダー

school uniform

制服

uniform

ユニフォーム

bib
よだれかけ

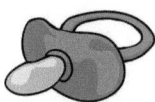

dummy
おしゃぶり

nappy
おむつ

office
オフィス

server
サーバ

filing cabinet
書類キャビネット

printer
プリンター

paper
紙

monitor
モニター

mouse
マウス

desk
事務机

folder
フォルダー

keyboard
キーボード

chair
椅子

waste-paper basket
ごみ箱

computer
コンピューター

coffee mug
コーヒーマグ

calculator
計算機

internet
インターネット

laptop
ラップトップ

letter
手紙

message
メッセージ

mobile
携帯電話

network
ネットワーク

photocopier
コピー機

software
ソフトウェア

telephone
電話

plug socket
コンセント

fax machine
ファックス

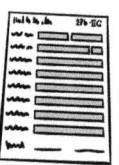

form
フォーム

document
書類

buy

買う

pay

支払う

trade

取引する

money

お金

dollar

ドル

euro

ユーロ

yen

円

rouble

ルーブル

Swiss franc

スイスフラン

renminbi yuan

人民元

rupee

ルピー

cashpoint

キャッシュポイント

bureau de change

両替所

gold

金

silver

銀

oil

油

energy

エネルギー

price

価格

contract

契約

tax

税金

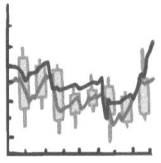

stock

株

work

働く

employee

従業員

employer

雇用主

factory

工場

shop

ショップ

occupations

職業

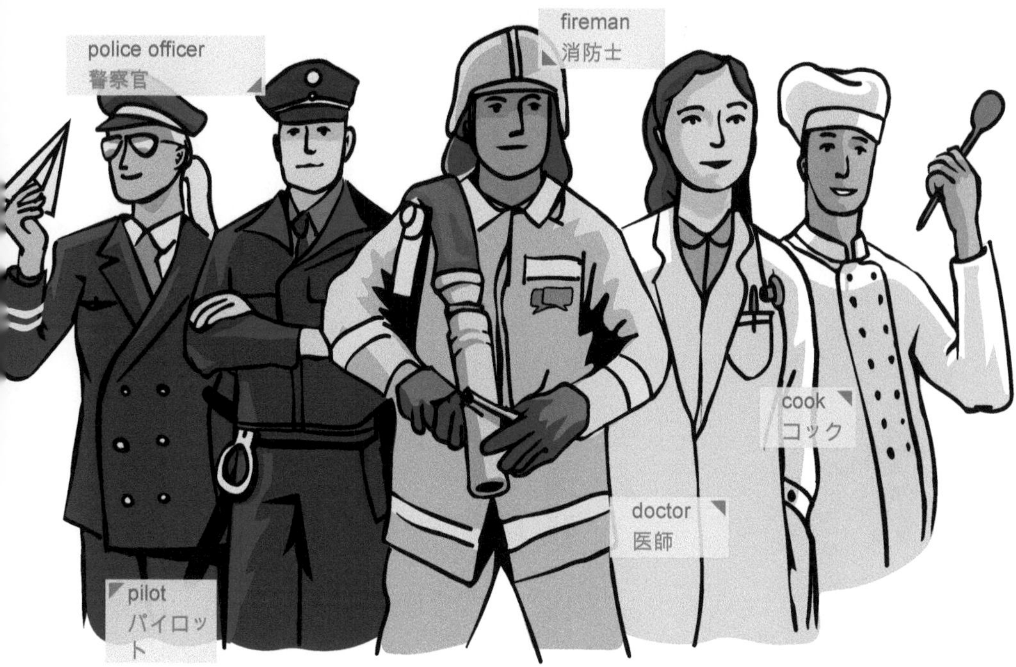

police officer
警察官
fireman
消防士
cook
コック
doctor
医師
pilot
パイロット

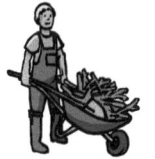

gardener

庭師

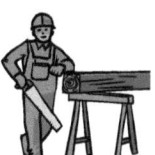

carpenter

大工

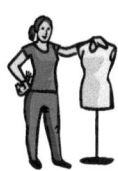

seamstress

お針子

judge

裁判官

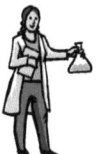

chemist

化学者

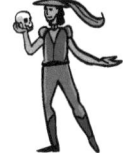

actor

俳優

bus driver

バスの運転手

taxi driver

タクシー運転手

fisherman

漁師

cleaning lady

掃除婦

roofer

屋根ふき職人

waiter

ウェイター

hunter

ハンター

painter

塗装工

baker

パン屋

electrician

電気工

builder

建設作業員

engineer

エンジニア

butcher

肉屋

plumber

配管工

postman

郵便配達人

soldier

軍人

architect

建築家

cashier

レジ係

florist

花屋

hairdresser

美容師

conductor

車掌

mechanic

機械工

captain

キャプテン

dentist

歯科医

scientist

科学者

rabbi

ラビ

imam

イスラム導師

monk

修道士

clergyman

牧師

tools
道具

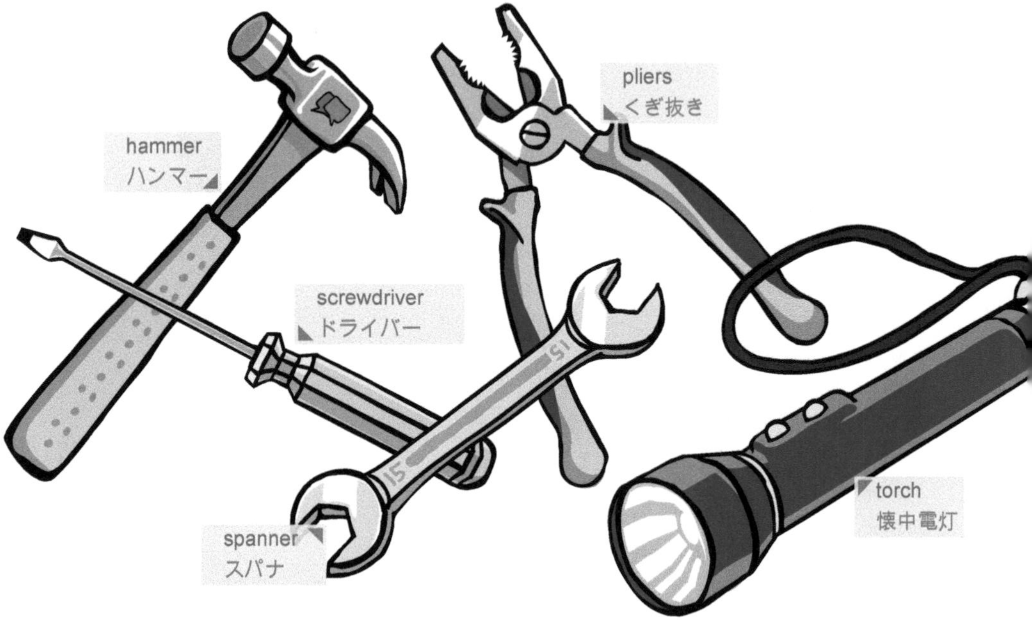
hammer
ハンマー
pliers
くぎ抜き
screwdriver
ドライバー
spanner
スパナ
torch
懐中電灯

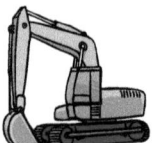

digger

掘削機

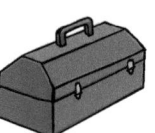

toolbox

道具箱

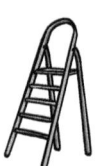

ladder

はしご

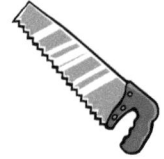

saw

のこぎり

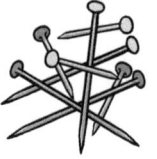

nails

釘

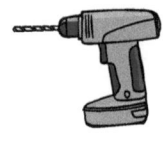

drill

ドリル

repair

修理する

shovel

シャベル

Damn!

クソ！

dustpan

ちりとり

paint pot

ペンキ缶

screws

ネジ

musical instruments

楽器

loudspeaker
スピーカー

drum kit
打楽器

guitar
ギター

double bass
コントラバス

trumpet
トランペ
ット

piano

ピアノ

violin

バイオリン

bass

バス

timpani

ティンパニ

drums

ドラム

keyboard

キーボード

saxophone

サックス

flute

フルート

microphone

マイクロフォン

ZOO

動物園

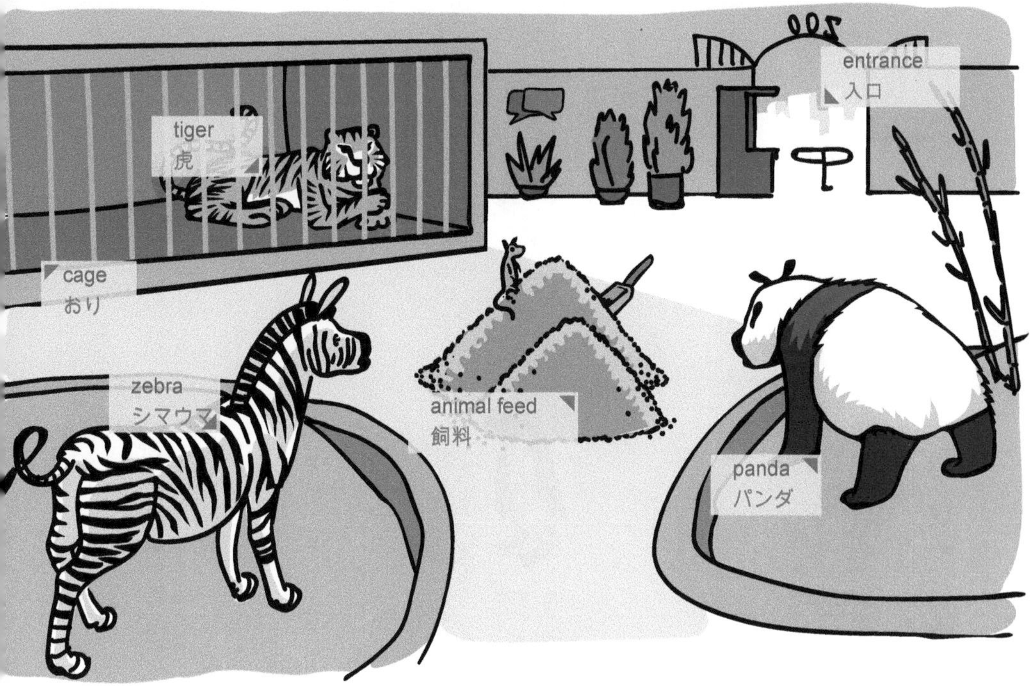
tiger
虎
cage
おり
entrance
入口
zebra
シマウマ
animal feed
飼料
panda
パンダ

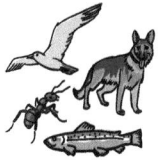

animals

動物

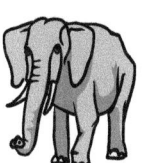

elephant

象

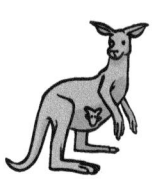

kangaroo

カンガルー

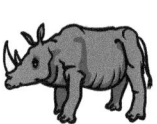

rhino

サイ

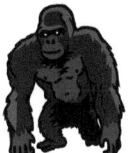

gorilla

ゴリラ

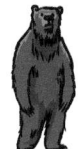

bear

熊

camel

ラクダ

ostrich

ダチョウ

lion

ライオン

monkey

猿

flamingo

フラミンゴ

parrot

オウム

polar bear

白クマ

penguin

ペンギン

shark

サメ

peacock

クジャク

snake

蛇

crocodile

ワニ

zookeeper

飼育係

seal

アザラシ

jaguar

ジャガー

pony

ポニー

leopard

ヒョウ

hippo

カバ

giraffe

キリン

eagle

鷲

boar

雄豚

fish

魚

turtle

亀

walrus

セイウチ

fox

狐

gazelle

ガゼル

American football
アメフト

cycling
サイクリング

tennis
テニス

basketball
バスケットボール

swimming
水泳

boxing
ボクシング

ice hockey
アイスホッケー

football
サッカー

badminton
バドミントン

athletics
陸上競技

handball
ハンドボール

skiing
スキー

polo
ポロ

jump
跳ぶ

laugh
笑う

hug
抱きしめる

walk
歩く

sing
歌う

dream
夢見る

pray
祈る

kiss
キス

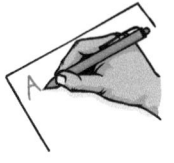

write
書く

draw
描く

show
示す

push
押す

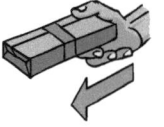

give
与える

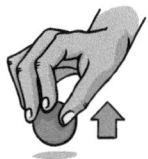

take
取る

have

持っている

do

する

be

ある

stand

立つ

run

走る

pull

引く

throw

投げる

fall

落ちる

lie

横たわっている

wait

待つ

carry

運ぶ

sit

座る

get dressed

着る

sleep

眠る

wake up

目が覚める

look at

見る

cry

泣く

stroke

なでる

comb

櫛ですく

talk

話す

understand

理解する

ask

質問する

listen

聞く

drink

飲む

eat

食べる

tidy up

片づける

love

愛する

cook

料理する

drive

運転する

fly

飛ぶ

sail
ヨットに乗る

calculate
計算する

read
読む

learn
学ぶ

work
働く

marry
結婚する

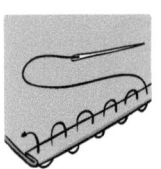

sew
縫う

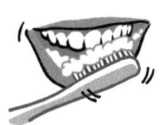

brush teeth
歯を磨く

kill
殺す

smoke
喫煙する

send
送る

family

家族

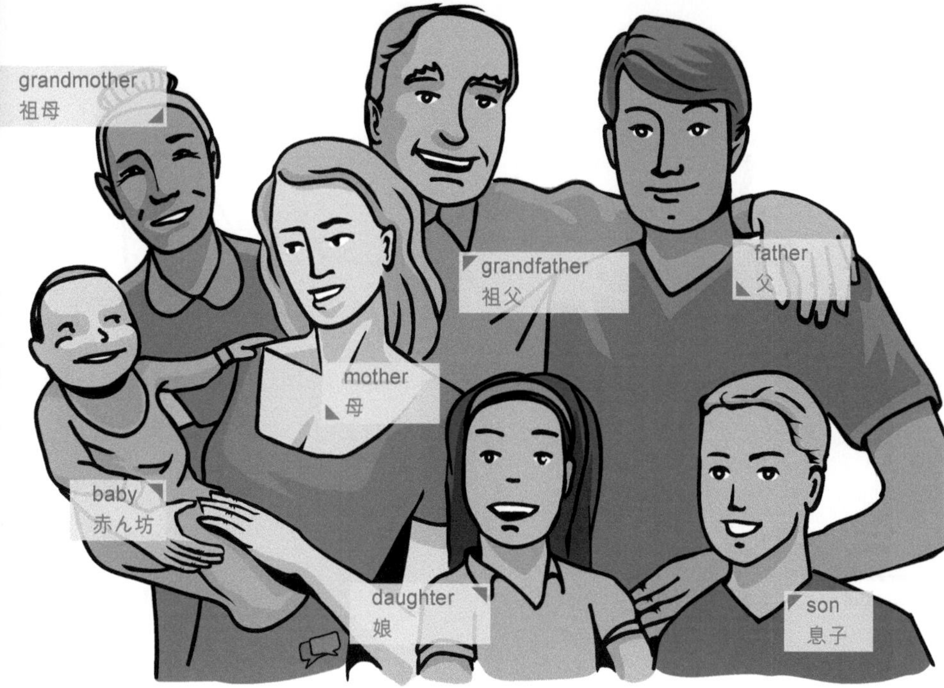

grandmother
祖母
grandfather
祖父
father
父
mother
母
baby
赤ん坊
daughter
娘
son
息子

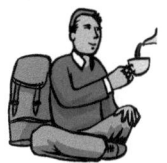

guest

お客様

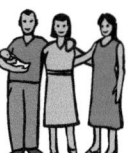

aunt

おば

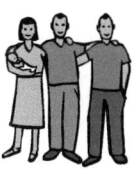

uncle

おじ

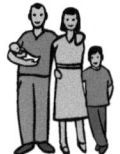

brother

兄弟

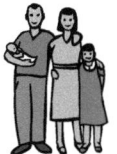

sister

姉妹

body

体

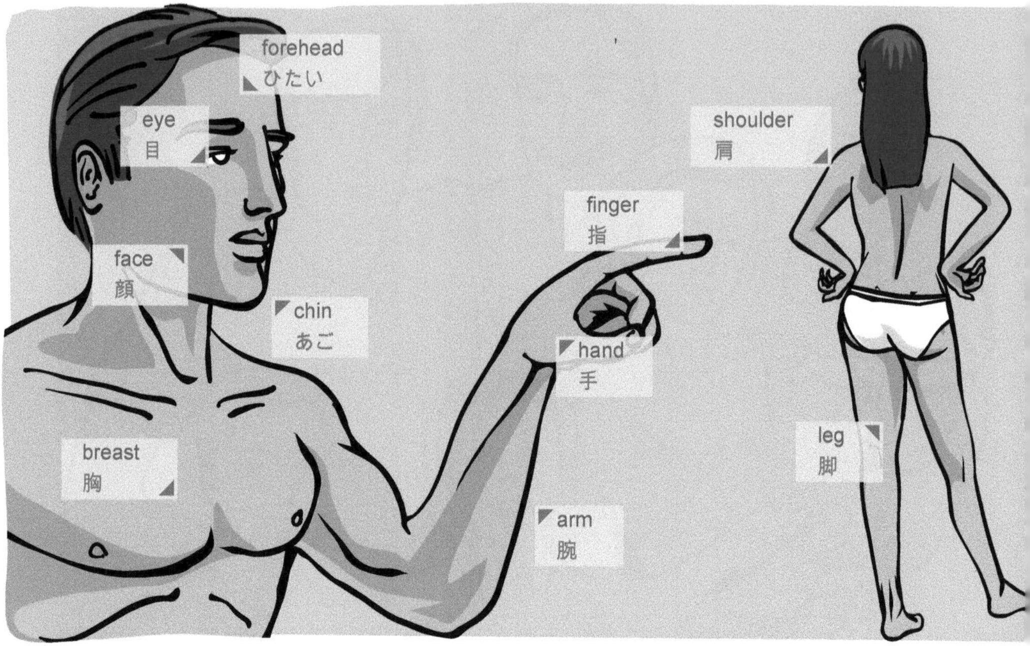

forehead
ひたい

eye
目

shoulder
肩

finger
指

face
顔

chin
あご

hand
手

breast
胸

leg
脚

arm
腕

baby

赤ん坊

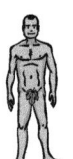

man

男性

woman

女性

girl

少女

boy

少年

head

頭

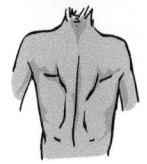

back

背中

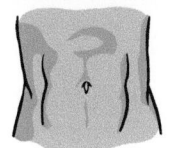

belly

腹

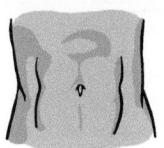

belly button

へそ

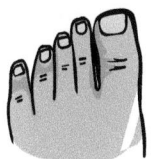

toe

足指

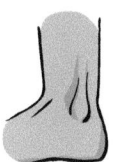

heel

かかと

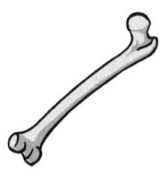

bone

骨

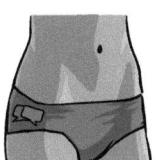

hip

腰

knee

ひざ

elbow

ひじ

nose

鼻

bottom

尻

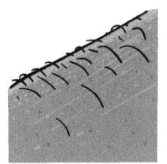

skin

皮膚

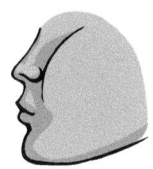

cheek

頬

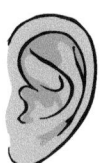

ear

耳

lip

唇

mouth

口

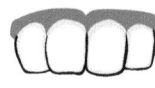

tooth

歯

tongue

舌

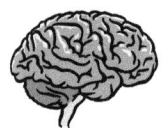

brain

脳

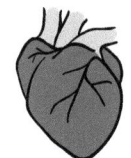

heart

心臓

muscle

筋肉

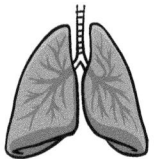

lung

肺

liver

肝臓

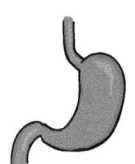

stomach

胃

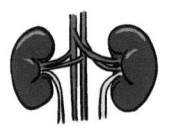

kidneys

腎臓

sex

セックス

condom

コンドーム

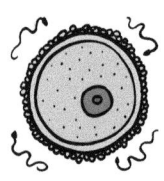

ovum

卵細胞

semen

精液

pregnancy

妊娠

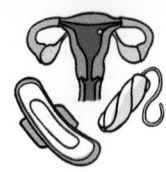

menstruation

月経

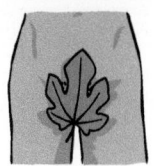

vagina

膣

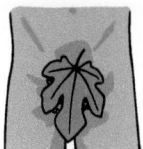

penis

ペニス

eyebrow

眉

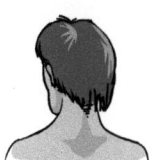

hair

髪

neck

首

hospital
病院

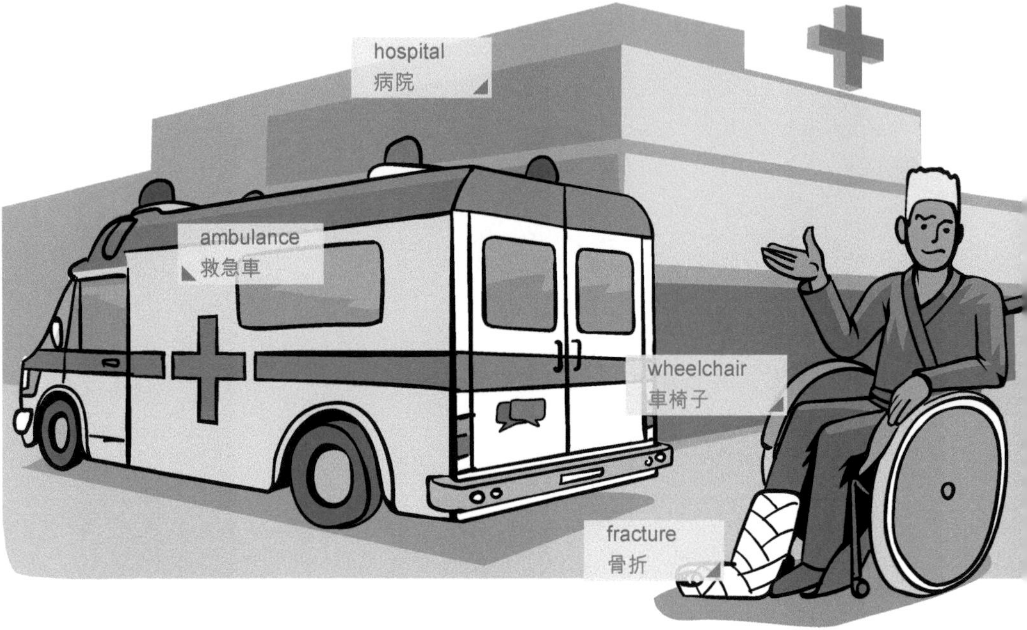

hospital
病院
ambulance
救急車
wheelchair
車椅子
fracture
骨折

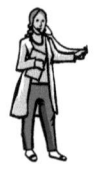

doctor

医師

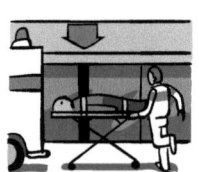

emergency room

救急治療室

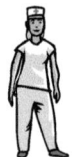

nurse

看護師

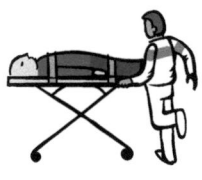

emergency

救急

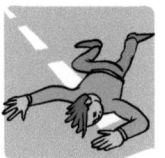

unconscious

失神

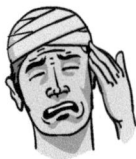

pain

痛み

injury

けが

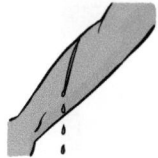

bleeding

出血

heart attack

心臓発作

stroke

脳卒中

allergy

アレルギー

cough

咳

fever

熱

flu

インフルエンザ

diarrhoea

下痢

headache

頭痛

cancer

癌

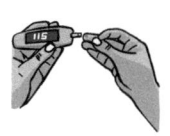

diabetes

糖尿病

surgeon

外科医

scalpel

外科用メス

operation

手術

CT

CT

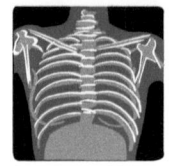

x-ray

レントゲン

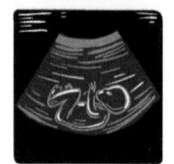

ultrasound

超音波

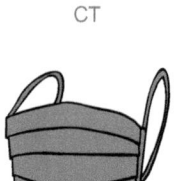

face mask

マスク

disease

病気

waiting room

待合室

crutch

松葉づえ

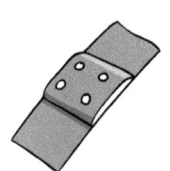

plaster

ばんそうこう

bandage

包帯

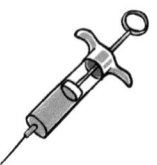

injection

注射

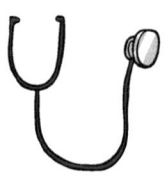

stethoscope

聴診器

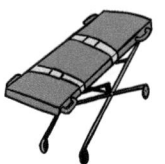

stretcher

担架

clinical thermometer

体温計

birth

出産

overweight

肥満

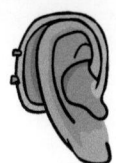

hearing aid

補聴器

disinfectant

消毒剤

infection

感染

virus

ウイルス

HIV / AIDS

HIV / エイズ

medicine

内服薬

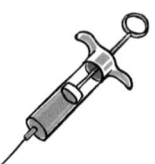

vaccination

予防接種

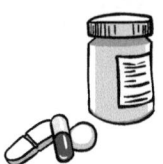

tablets

錠剤

pill

ピル

emergency call

緊急電話

blood pressure monitor

血圧計

ill / healthy

病気の　/　健康な

Help!

助けて！

alarm

アラーム

assault

暴行

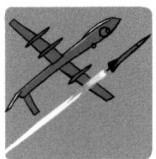

attack

攻撃

danger

危険

emergency exit

非常口

Fire!

火事だ！

fire extinguisher

消火器

accident

事故

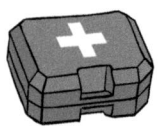

first-aid kit

救急箱

SOS

SOS

police

警察

Europe

ヨーロッパ

North America

北米

South America

南米

Africa

アフリカ

Asia

アジア

Australia

オーストラリア

Atlantic

大西洋

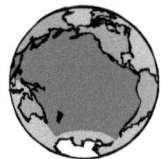

Pacific

太平洋

Indian Ocean

インド洋

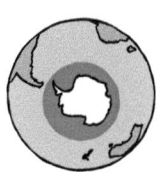

Antarctic Ocean

南極海

Arctic Ocean

北極海

North Pole

北極

South Pole
南極

Antarctica
南極大陸

Earth
地球

land
陸

sea
海

island
島

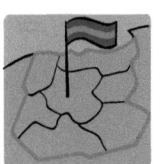

nation
国家

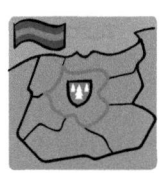

state
国家

clock face

文字盤

hour hand

短針

minute hand

長針

second hand

秒針

What time is it?

何時ですか？

day

日

time

時間

now

現在

digital watch

デジタル時計

minute

分

hour

時間

week

週

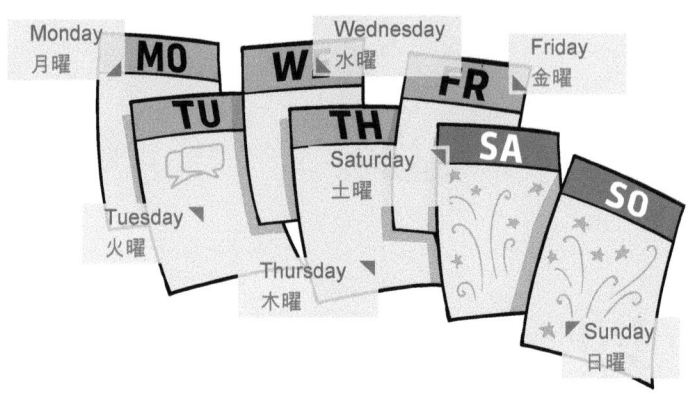

Monday
月曜

Wednesday
水曜

Friday
金曜

Tuesday
火曜

Thursday
木曜

Saturday
土曜

Sunday
日曜

yesterday

昨日

today

今日

tomorrow

明日

morning

朝

noon

昼

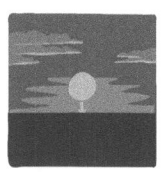

evening

夜

business days

營業日

weekend

週末

year

年

rain
雨
wind
風
snow
雪
spring
春
autumn
秋
summer
夏
winter
冬

4.APRIL 11°
5.APRIL 4°
6.APRIL 13°
7.APRIL 8°
8.APRIL 10°

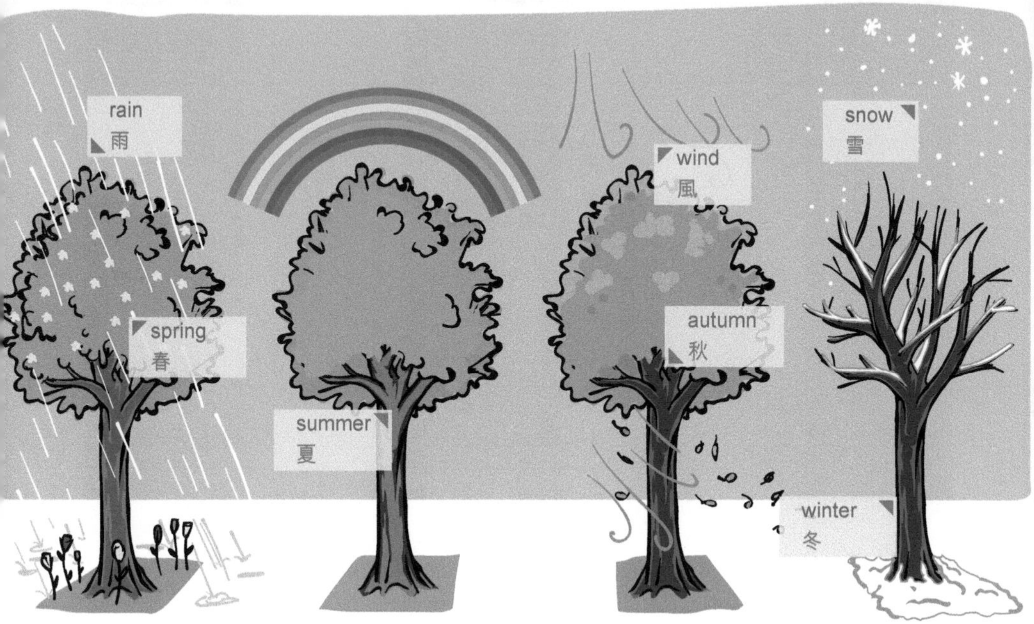

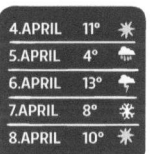

weather forecast

天気予報

F C
120 40
90 30
60 20
30 10
0 0
-30 -10
-20

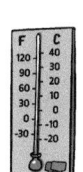

thermometer

温度計

sunshine

日差し

cloud

雲

fog

霧

humidity

湿度

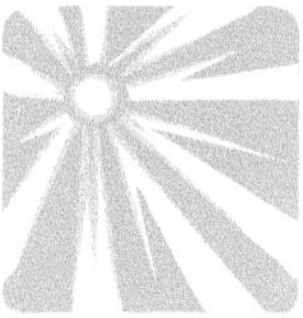

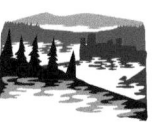

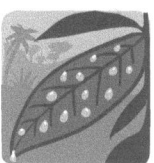

lightning

雷

thunder

雷

storm

嵐

hail

ひょう

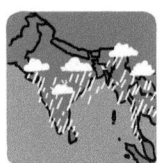

monsoon

季節風

flood

洪水

ice

氷

January

1月

February

2月

March

3月

April

4月

May

5月

June

6月

July

7月

August

8月

year - 年

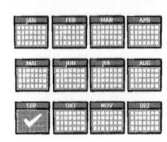

September

9月

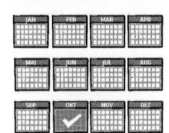

October

10月

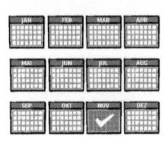

November

11月

December

12月

shapes

形

circle

円

square

正方形

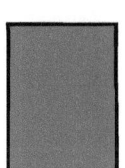

rectangle

長方形

triangle

三角

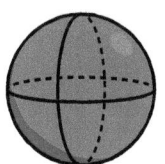

sphere

球

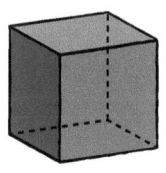

cube

立方体

colours

色

white

白

yellow

黄

orange

オレンジ

pink

ピンク

red

赤

purple

紫

blue

青

green

緑

brown

茶

grey

灰色

black

黒

a lot / a little

多い / 少ない

angry / calm

怒っている /
落ち着いている

beautiful / ugly

美しい / 醜い

beginning / end

初め / 終わり

big / small

大きい / 小さい

bright / dark

明るい / 暗い

brother / sister

兄弟 / 姉妹

clean / dirty

清潔な / 汚い

complete / incomplete

完全な / 不完全な

day / night

日中 / 夜

dead / alive

死んだ / 生きている

wide / narrow

幅広い / 狭い

edible / inedible

食べられる /
食べられない

evil / kind

悪意のある / 親切な

excited / bored

興奮している /
退屈している

fat / thin

太った / 痩せた

first / last

最初に / 最後に

friend / enemy

友人 / 敵

full / empty

いっぱいの / 空の

hard / soft

硬い / 柔らかい

heavy / light

重い / 軽い

hunger / thirst

空腹 / 喉の渇き

ill / healthy

病気の / 健康な

illegal / legal

違法な / 合法な

intelligent / stupid

賢い / 愚かな

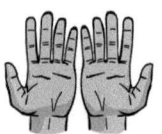

left / right

左に / 右に

near / far

近い / 遠い

new / used

新しい ／ 中古の

nothing / something

何もない ／ 何かある

old / young

老いた ／ 若い

on / off

オン ／ オフ

open / closed

開いている ／
閉まっている

quiet / loud

静かな ／ うるさい

rich / poor

裕福な ／ 貧乏な

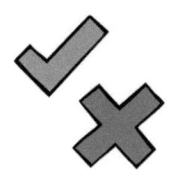

right / wrong

正しい ／ 間違っている

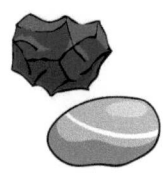

rough / smooth

粗い ／ なめらか

sad / happy

悲しい ／ 幸せな

short / long

短い ／ 長い

slow / fast

ゆっくり ／ 速い

wet / dry

濡れた ／ 乾いた

warm / cool

温かい ／ 冷たい

war / peace

戦争 ／ 平和

0

zero

ゼロ

1

one

1

2

two

2

3

three

3

4

four

4

5

five

5

6

six

6

7

seven

7

8

eight

8

9

nine

9

10

ten

10

11

eleven

11

12

twelve

12

13

thirteen

13

14

fourteen

14

15

fifteen

15

16

sixteen

16

17

seventeen

17

18

eighteen

18

19

nineteen

19

20

twenty

20

100

hundred

100

1.000

thousand

1000

1.000.000

million

100万

English

英語

American English

アメリカ英語

Chinese Mandarin

中国標準語

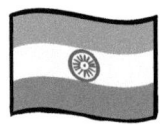

Hindi

ヒンディー語

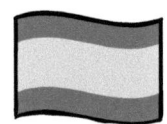

Spanish

スペイン語

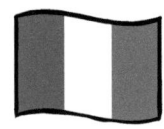

French

フランス語

Arabic

アラビア語

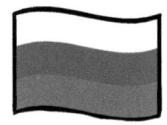

Russian

ロシア語

Portuguese

ポルトガル語

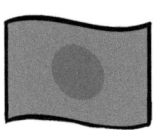

Bengali

ベンガル語

German

ドイツ語

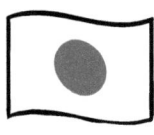

Japanese

日本語

I

私

you

あなた

he / she / it

彼 ／ 彼女 ／ それ

we

私たち

you

あなたたち

they

彼ら

who?

誰？

what?

何？

how?

どうやって？

where?

どこ？

when?

いつ？

name

名前

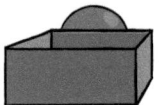

behind

後ろ

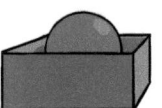

in

中

in front of

前

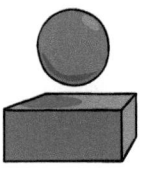

over

上

on

上

under

下

beside

横

between

間

place

場所